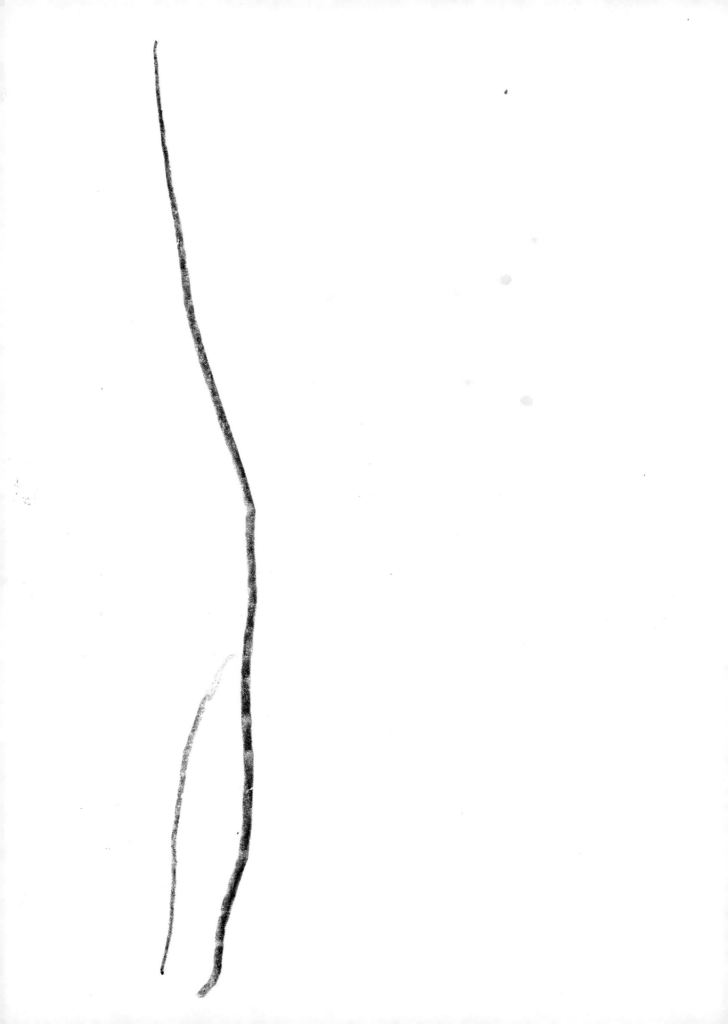

SANTA ARE YOU FOR REAL?

written by
Harold Myra

illustrated by
Dwight Walles

THOMAS NELSON INC., PUBLISHERS

Nashville   New York

A word to Parents, Grandparents, Aunts, Uncles . . .

Christmas, children, and Santa Claus. The combination often generates adult explosions against materialism and the bearded, jolly Mr. Claus crowding out the Christ Child. Why, the argument goes, should children be so self-centered, so caught up with a myth which distorts Christmas into a push-shove pagan holiday?

Why indeed? I had always been ambivalent myself. But then I read about St. Nicholas of Myra.* Even after skimming off the tall tales about him and adjusting for medieval exaggeration, he comes up as a rather exciting person for children to know about. It's important they understand the roots of the Santa Claus phenomenon, and how clearly the original St. Nick put the Christ Child at the heart of *his* Christmas.

—Harold Myra

*Nicholas became bishop in the seaport of Myra, a city mentioned in the Bible (no connection with the author, who is of Norwegian descent).

For TODD STEPHEN MYRA,
who, at five, still believes.

Published in Nashville, Tennessee, by Thomas Nelson, Inc., Publishers and distributed in Canada by Lawson Falle, Ltd., Cambridge, Ontario.

Printed in the United States of America.

Fourth Printing

ISBN 0-8407-5122-2

'Twas the night before Christmas,
and out on the street,
a wee boy was standing,
big boots on his feet.

He stamped them, and kicked them,
threw snow at a rock
to crowd out the songs
of the kids on his block.

3

Hey, Hey, Hey,
he heard them say,
Santa's phony—all the way!
Oh what fun
to jump and run
and laugh about his sleigh
Hey!

Todd stamped with his boots—
stamped harder and louder,
But couldn't be noisy—
the snow was just powder.

Santa's a fake,
just a guy in a store.
It's Dad who brings presents—
he sneaks through the door!

5

But suddenly, then,
the kids saw Todd's face,
all troubled and sad,
staring out into space.

"Well, maybe he's real
for a twerp small as you,"
said Peter, in fourth grade,
who certainly knew.
"You can think ole St. Nick
will bring you those toys,
and try to be one
of his good little boys.
But don't look for us
to go giggling around.
On roof tops tonight,
we expect not a sound!"

Todd's sister Michelle,
who was wiser and older
(as old as first grade,
so just a bit bolder)
had watched the whole scene
and pulled Todd away
as she said some kind words
for old Santa and sleigh.

Now sometimes, you see,
the girl and her brother
would fight and complain
and upset their mother.
But this was a time
of compassion and love,
as a caring Michelle
reached out with her glove
and patted his cheek
(though she got it all snowy)
and told him the kids
were full of baloney.

Then they huddled so close,
they merged in the snowflakes,
and she told him about
Mommy's cookies and fruitcakes.
She whispered quite softly,
scrunched down to his size,
"Tonight's Christmas Eve!"
Lights danced in her eyes.

But Todd gave a snort
and whirled through the snow.
He kicked at the flakes—
didn't anyone know?
Santa's a fake!
He tromped back inside
and tried to start playing . . .
but something had died.

Dad watched Todd come in,
saw his face was all glum,
so he bent down and asked,
"What's the matter, old chum?"
Todd plopped on the sofa,
and let out a sigh.
He certainly was not,
was **not** going to cry!
He stared at his dad
and wrinkled his face.
"No Santa or reindeer
will come to our place!
The chimney's too skinny,
he can't really fly.
He's not at the North Pole.
It's all a big lie!"

Todd's face was all tense;
he was clenching his fists.
His lips were tight white;
he kept twisting his wrists.
Dad reached for the boy,
pulled him tight to his side,
and kissed him and told him,
"Let's see, Todd, who's lied."

"Now, where would one start
about jolly St. Nick?"
But Todd barely listened,
suspecting a trick.
If grownups told stories
that just weren't so,
then how could he trust them?
How could he know?

"Let's start all 'way back
when St. Nick was born—
"But he's just pretend!"
Todd felt angry and torn.
"Oh, no," Dad insisted,
"He was born just like us,
before the first jet,
or first car or bus."

Back, back, back . . . to learn
of St. Nicholas, you have to
go back before he was born,
to a stable in Bethlehem. It's
the first Christmas!

"Joy to the world! The Lord
is come!"

Baby Jesus was very, very
special. You see, God saw
that people were selfish,
proud, and cruel. So God
came to earth as a baby.

13

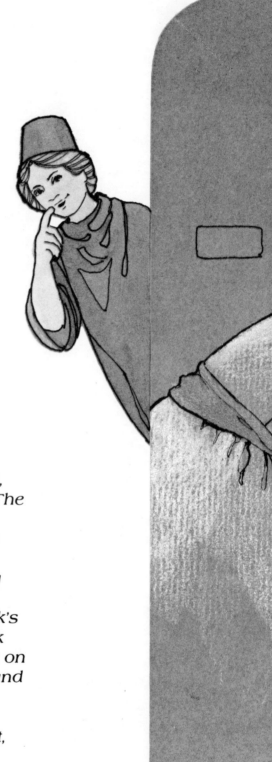

Jesus grew up. He showed people how to live, and how to obey God. And then He died on a cross so that God could forgive our sins.

Joy to the world! That's what Christmas is all about. The Savior is come! And that's the beginning of Santa, too . . . .

You see, after Jesus rose from the dead, His friends spread the word about Him. The Apostle Paul carried the Good News to a country named Lycia. And less than 300 years later, a baby was born there.

The baby's name was Nicholas. Young Nick grew up to love Jesus very much. When he was nine years old, both of Nick's parents died. But he wasn't bitter. He took his love for his parents and poured it out on people around him, especially the poor and needy.

Nicholas loved to obey Jesus and give gifts. Only he gave them secretly, at night, because he wasn't looking for thanks.

My favorite story about Nicholas happened when he was a teenager. We're not sure of all the details, but here's how I first heard it.

Nick knew a kind man with three lovely daughters. Each girl loved a young man. Each wanted to get married. But in those days, a girl had to have money—a "dowry"—before a wedding could be announced.

The father was very poor. Things got so bad that one girl was going to sell herself so the others could marry.

When Nick heard about this, he put some money into a bag and quietly, while it was dark, walked to their house.

A window was open. He tossed the money into the oldest girl's room, and it fell into a stocking hung there to dry. Nick then quietly left.

The father and daughters were delighted. The oldest girl had a marvelous wedding, and everyone wondered who had given the gift. Later, on another night, Nick did the same thing. And so, the second girl got married, and she was very happy. But who had helped them, they wondered.

There was one girl left. Would she
miss out?

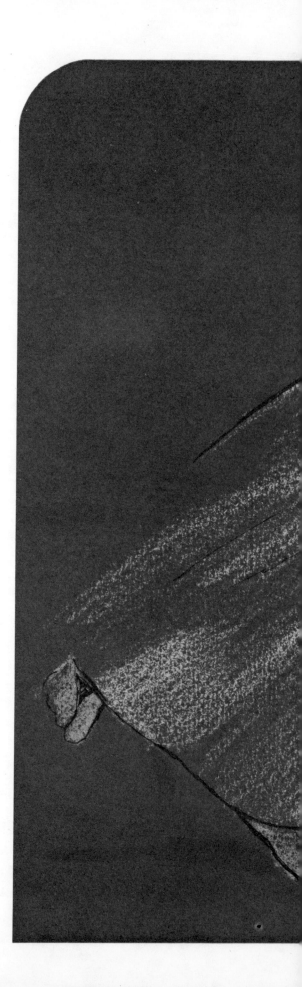

On another dark night, Nick sneaked up to her house and tossed in a third bag of gold. But this time the father heard him! He rushed to the door and bolted outside. Nick realized he had been seen and tried to dash away. But the father ran and caught up to him.

He recognized Nick and he smiled. The father thanked him for making it possible for his daughters to get married, but Nick asked him not to tell anyone else. "Keep my secret," he asked. And the father did. For years after that, no one knew who had helped them.

Nick was like that—always helping people, but never looking for thanks. He loved Jesus so much he soon became a bishop in the church. He kept doing kind things for people, and even when he was thrown into jail for being a Christian, he wouldn't give up his love for Jesus.

After he died, people eventually called him a saint, because that's what someone is who loves God so much. Over the years, people remembered St. Nicholas and how he gave gifts. In Holland they call him *Sinterclaas,* in England *Father Christmas,* in France *Père Nöel, and here we call him* **Santa Claus.**

*Of course, some children know
all about Santa, and presents,
and reindeer, but forget all about
Jesus. To St. Nick, that would
ruin Christmas! Jesus was Nick's
whole life.*

*You see, the real St. Nicholas is
now in heaven with Jesus. And
all the Santas you see in stores
and on sidewalks remind us of
St. Nicholas and the reason he
gave gifts—because Jesus came
the first Christmas, to give
Himself for us.*

Todd snuggled up close,
for he'd missed not a word.
Now he stared at the chimney,
thinking through what he'd heard.

"There won't be a sleigh
on my rooftop tonight,
and no Rudolph," he said,
"with nose glowing bright.
But I'm going to do
what Nick was about.
I'm going to give gifts
and not be found out!"

Todd ran up the stairs,
his face full of scheming.
A long time went by
till he came back all beaming.
His arms were both full
of oddly wrapped boxes.
"I wrapped up my nickels,
and one of my foxes."

Stuffed toys and a dump truck,
a clown with one leg—
all wrapped for Michelle
and for one-year-old Greg.

Todd piled them up high
by the tree lighted bright,
and then he announced,
"Santa's been here tonight!"

His daddy just laughed
as he lifted the boy.
"That's wonderful, Todd—
to share gives us joy.
The stories of reindeer,
of snowflakes, and elves
are holiday magic,
when we think past ourselves."

"I'll act like St. Nick,"
Todd said to his dad,
**"It's Jesus he loved—
He makes us all glad!"**

So they all sat around
and they talked half the night,
while Todd thought he saw,
in the snow and moonlight,
a bright-eyed St. Nicholas,
with his sack, looking in,
and wide 'cross his face,
a jolly old grin.

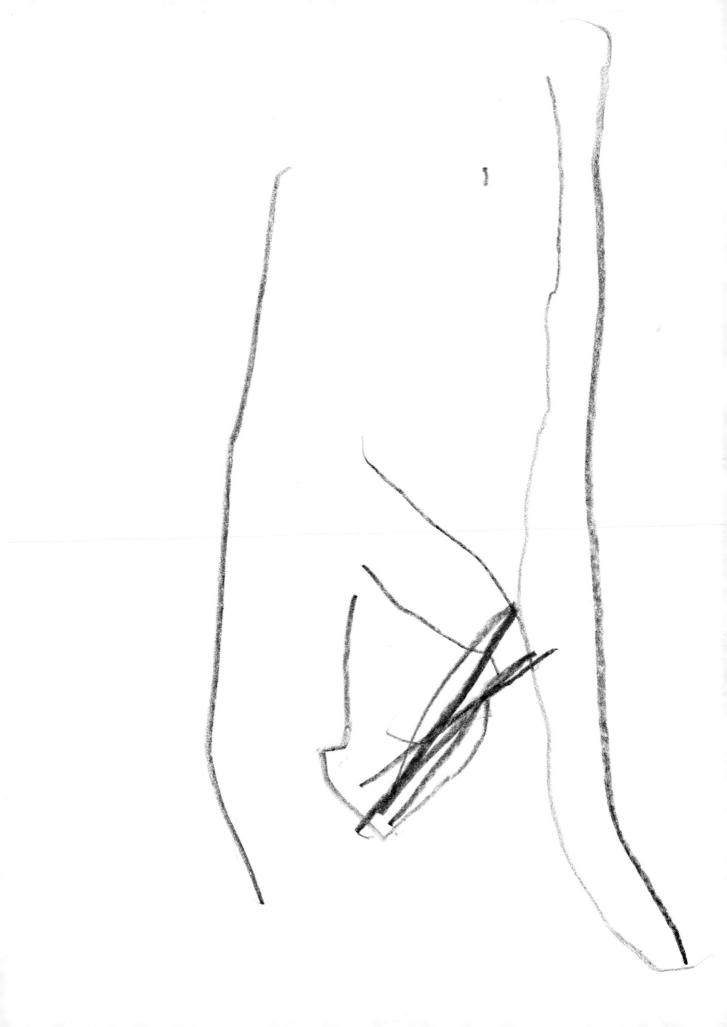